BUDDHISM FOR DUDES

D1166793

Buddhism for Dudes

A JARHEAD'S FIELD GUIDE TO MINDFULNESS

GERRY STRIBLING

Wisdom Publications
199 Elm Street
Somerville, MA 02144 USA
wisdompubs.org

Library of Congress Cataloging-in-Publication Data
Stribling, Gerry, author.
  Buddhism for dudes / Gerry Stribling.
      pages cm
  ISBN 1-61429-229-9 (pbk. : alk. paper)
  1. Buddhism. 2. Buddhists—Religious life. I. Title.
  BQ4132.S76 2015
  294.3—dc23
                            2014047476

ISBN 978-1-61429-229-6   eBook ISBN 978-1-61429-244-9

19 18 17 16 15
5 4 3 2 1

Cover design by Philip Pascuzzo. Interior design by Gopa&Ted2, Inc. Set in The Serif SemiLight 10/16. Artwork by Ivette Salom.

Wisdom Publications' books are printed on acid-free paper and meet the guidelines for permanence and durability of the Production Guidelines for Book Longevity of the Council on Library Resources.

This book was produced with environmental mindfulness. We have elected to print this title on 30% PCW recycled paper. As a result, we have saved the following resources: 6 trees, 3 million BTUs of energy, 493 lbs. of greenhouse gases, 2,670 gallons of water, and 179 lbs. of solid waste. For more information, please visit our website, wisdompubs.org.

Printed in the United States of America.

For Nanda

Contents

Introduction

When I traveled to Sri Lanka as a volunteer after the World Trade Center went down on September 11, 2001, I wanted to show all my scaredy-cat friends back home that the only thing they had to fear was... fear itself. My original destination was Pakistan. But given the climate in Pakistan at the time, I figured my chances of being beheaded that summer would be significantly less in Sri Lanka.

And so terrorism had a hand in creating this book, because my change of venue gave me the great good fortune, quite by accident, to study the wisdom of Buddhism with monks, forty of them, in fact, ranging in age from ten to eighty. Studying with them on their home turf was especially delightful—after dark, in the less stifling heat of night, the smell of incense and lamp oil and jasmine, and the occasional raucous cry of a peacock back in the jungle, sitting on low benches so that I was seated at cobra level, lower than the monks. I spent many months literally sitting at the feet of my mentors, some of them the most eminent Buddhist thinkers in South Asia, and even at the feet of the eleven-year-old novice who taught me how to chant.

Sri Bodhiraja Monastery, like the U.S. Marines, is a fairly regimented and gender-specific environment. It just so happens that my two periods of greatest personal growth were in times and places where everyone around me was male, and everybody wore the same outfits. What did I learn from them? The Marines teach self-sacrifice and monks teach—and live—the secret of life, which is to enjoy self-sacrifice. That's why monks are happy guys. I learned how to step up for others from the Marines and how to be happy from my monk friends. Having lived in both of these worlds, my experience is that these two ways of life fold seamlessly into one another.

But don't take my word for it. Out of all the people who ever wrote a book in an attempt to interpret Buddhist wisdom, I am probably the worst example of a Buddhist. I think I'm a pretty good Buddhist, but so many who came before me are, well, holy men. I've met a few holy men, and I'm not one of them. There isn't a precept I haven't broken or a spiritual goal that I have fully attained. So: *do not take my word for anything.*

Know who else said that? The Buddha.

I merrily stumble my way down the Middle Path, as the teachings are sometimes called, because it makes me sane. When you start stripping away the nonsense stuck in your head, all the bad learning and misplaced priorities, and you poke your head out the door to take an honest look at the world, you can see just what a dismal place full of agony and suffering the world is.

But here's the thing! Fortunately, seeing the truth has a way of setting you free. It can even vaccinate you against the horrors we face in life and show you how to be basically happy.

Personally, I love to be happy. Oh, sure, I get a case of the red-ass every now and then, but generally and genuinely happy I am, and happy I intend to stay. Buddhism has a lot to offer in terms of wisdom that can get you through the hardest parts of life, and that can generally make you happy to be alive no matter what.

So here you have it, in an easy-to-carry format: Gerry the Jarhead's take on Buddhist wisdom for the Average Joe, a take heavy on the info and light on the metaphysics. Here I share a secret mystery of life with guys who only read books during the off-season. You know: guys who head for the gambling boat when there's a big welterweight fight on so they can reinvest the money they *would* have spent watching it at home on pay-per-view; guys with bumper stickers on the back of their pickups that say, "A bad day fishing is better than a good day working."

Get it? This is not a book written with women in mind. I'm not trying to be sexist by not considering women's perspectives. If you're a woman, you are quite welcome to read this book. But I'm basically clueless about women; I know that I'm not qualified to write for women. I've been married to one for forty years, but that doesn't mean that I actually know anything about women. I'm only a guy.

Know who else said "I'm only a guy"? The Buddha!

1
Buddhism, No Bullshit

There is a healthy, reasonable way of living, a simple philosophy that people mistake for a religion, which is a recipe for both world peace and personal sanity. It's called Buddhism, and it's hardly new; the Buddha lived five hundred years before Jesus was born. In a very real way, Buddhism is pretty easy to understand—yet many people think that it is mysterious and inscrutable. There are some pretty wacky misconceptions about Buddhism out there, but it can become a real support system for those of us who just don't otherwise get the point of modern life.

If you Google "Buddhism" and start clicking on sites, you're going to encounter a confusing array of ideas, writings—and plenty of bullshit.

Most images of the Buddha have fit, studlier bodies
with a round head of curly hair tied in a top-knot.

The nitty-gritty stuff you really need to know to understand Buddhism and explore how following the Buddhist path can improve your life—well, dude, that's harder to find.

Americans tend to have a skewed conception of Buddhism. If you're over fifty, the indelible image seared in your mind from the Buddhist world may be the monk who set himself on fire in Saigon to protest the Vietnam War. Under fifty and you probably picture the Dalai Lama. Some people see Buddhism as an "Asian thing" inaccessible to Americans except for overeducated, vegan, antiwar whale huggers and the like. Misconceptions and partial information tend to typify our idea of what Buddhism is.

Take, for example, the image of the Buddha himself, or at least the image many Americans associate with the founder of this philosophy: until I went to Asia, I didn't know that the Buddha was not a fat guy—the hairless bag-toting Santa Claus often seen in the front of Chinese restaurants wearing a shit-eating grin on his big, chubby face. That image is actually a Chinese god of happiness and contentment. Most images of the Buddha have fit, studlier bodies with a round head of curly hair tied in a top-knot. But when it comes down to it, what sets the Buddha apart isn't his appearance; it's what he taught.

My experience with Buddhism is focused on the hard-core basics of the belief system and their application in our professional and personal lives. Buddhism is good stuff. I want my fishing buddies to know about it. Everybody should know some Dharma. If they did, the world would be a more peaceful place.

Everything you need to know about basic, no-frills Buddhist wisdom can be outlined on a half-sheet of paper. There are three refuges, four noble truths, five precepts, and an eight-point guide to proper (and happy) living. You don't have to "go Asian" to understand Buddhism. You don't have to quit eating meat or drinking beer. The Buddha ate meat when that was what was offered to him, and a beer every now and then isn't going to get you into too much trouble.

Buddhism is all about being a stand-up guy, a *mensch*, someone who'll never let someone down. Buddhism is being secure and confident in your approach to life. I'm sure a lot of people benefit in many different ways from Buddhist wisdom—what many people don't understand is that *it's not about them*.

It takes guts to be a Buddhist dude. It's not about hiding in your own little world; it's about living and meeting all of life's challenges in a meaningful and unselfish way. It's about super-hero ethics, a soldier's devotion to duty, and the kind of happiness you come by only from being fearless. A significant contention of this book is that you don't have to surrender your manly fortitude to adopt Dharma into your life.

2

Who Was the Buddha?

More than twenty-five-hundred years ago in
northern India, a prince was born into a world
of great splendor and wealth. Siddhartha Gautama lived the lifestyle of the rich and famous.
His parents, intent on making sure the young
prince's life was as happy as possible, sheltered
him from the ugly realities of the world. In fact,
he was pushing thirty—with a wife and a kid, no
less—before he learned that people grow old, get
sick, and die. For a clueless but otherwise intelli-
gent guy to discover the cold, hard facts of life at
that late a stage was a real wake-up-call, a major
bombshell. "Suffering!" the prince realized. "The
human experience is about a lot of suffering.
Holy crap!"

Gautama became obsessed with finding out how to deal with the suffering he saw in the world. It was a pretty tall order, but somebody had to do it. He left the life of luxury (and also his wife and kid) and, like Willie Nelson, he hit the road—Gautama the Dharma bum. How many servicemen and women have had to make the same kind of sacrifice for the greater good? Karen Armstrong, a biographer of the Buddha, says that he probably agonized over that decision.

At first he sought out gurus in order to learn from them and to synthesize their wisdom. They disappointed him. He then tried living the life of an ascetic, an existence characterized by self-denial and self-imposed misery. Because he starved himself, he lost a lot of weight and even ended up near death, nothing but skin and bones. Finally, after giving it his best effort, and after eating a bowl of milk rice, Gautama figured out that such an austere existence was as stupid as his former royal life was decadent and mean- ingless. After experiencing the two extremes, he eventually realized that the truth was to be found somewhere in the middle between the two—a "middle path," if you will.

Gautama sat under a tree and started meditating, vowing to himself that he would not leave that spot until he figured it all out: *What is the purpose of existence? Why does life have to hurt so much? How should we live and deal with our suffering and with the suffering of our fellow human beings?* He sat under that tree for a long time. And then—WHAMMO! The final eureka smacked him upside the head and he achieved perfect understanding—enlightenment. He experienced such incredible bliss that he closed his eyes, tilted his head back, and wagged it back and forth from experiencing the joy of it all. He didn't stop, they say, for seven days. Tradition says otherwise, but I like to imagine that he felt just as if he'd struck gold at Sutter's Mill and had to go tell somebody.

He sought out five equally starved buddies in the park, guys who'd stuck with him through thick and thin, and he told them what he had discovered. That speech is now known as the Buddha's first sermon, or the "first turning of the Dharma Wheel." In it the Buddha expressed everything anyone ever needed to know in order to survive life and to achieve contentment and salvation. The Dharma, i.e., the wisdom that the Buddha shared with others for the next half-century, is handed down to us today. The essence of that wisdom is called the Four Noble Truths. Contained within the Four Noble Truths is the Noble Eightfold Path, a blueprint for living life the right way. And part of that blueprint is the Five Precepts, the Buddha's rules for living a stand-up life. (Something like a Buddhist version of the Ten Commandments. Although the analogy is imprecise, you get the idea.) All of Buddhist wisdom can be found in that first sermon. In an important sense, everything else the Buddha taught (and there's a lot of it) is commentary.

The Buddha was in his midthirties when he achieved perfect wisdom, and for the next fifty years he traveled all around northern India teaching what he learned for himself under the Bodhi Tree. He attracted a great many disciples and died in his eighties from food poisoning. If you ever travel the world and see statues of the Buddha and you see one lying down, that's the dying Buddha, felled by foul pork just like any ordinary man after a trip to a bad barbecue joint.

After all, that was all the Buddha ever claimed to be: an ordinary man.

After experiencing the two extremes, he eventually realized that the truth was to be found somewhere in the
middle between the two—a "middle path," if you will.

3

Is Buddhism a Religion or Not?

Now, the notion that the Buddha was *not* divine confused the heck out of me when I first took up residence at a Buddhist temple in Asia. I hung out exclusively in the company of monks for months, during which time I saw a lot of what looked to me a heck of a lot like religious rituals. Several times a day monks would chant what seemed to be prayers, and they frequently behaved toward statues in a way that any Orthodox Rabbi would call "bowing down to false idols."

Dozens of Buddha statues sat around the temple's campus, but the main one, the big guy in the shrine, was humongous—at least triple life-sized, and covered in gold. In many parts of Asia, you can't turn around without seeing a Buddha image—a little Buddha here, a big Buddha there, even Buddhas carved out of entire mountains. Every shop in Sri Lanka and Thailand has its own little shrine, and every home has one too. You'll encounter roadside Buddha shrines wherever you go. The Buddha is everywhere.

One night at the temple I had the chance to ask some fairly hot-shot Buddhist theologians about what the monks were up to during their services. Revealing my confusion, I asked, "If the Buddha was just a dude and not a god, then why do people bow down and pray to his image? What does all that worship have to do with Buddhism?"

Buddhism, I was informed, is not a religion. It is a moral philosophy. Buddhist "worship" isn't really worship, chanting isn't the same as prayer, and Buddha images are ubiquitous because we need to be reminded that there is a code of conduct to live by, and that *this* guy figured it out. When Buddhists sit before the Buddha's image they are reminded of the inner peace that they should enjoy if they live meditative, compassionate, and moral lives. The Buddha said that there was no reason to venerate him personally. His message is what's important.

By chanting we repeat the Buddha's message in order to remind ourselves of what we already know. Bowing and holding one's hands together in a prayerful way are Asian traditions. You see people make these gestures all the time over much of Asia, as well as any yoga class you might care to attend. To greet someone with a bow and your hands together is almost like shaking hands in the West, only there is an added element of reverence and respect. Showing respect is not worshipping. It's also more sanitary than shaking hands.

Most of us need ritual and tradition, even some form of "worship," if you want to call it that, whether we get it from religion or not. When it comes to ritual and tradition, NASCAR and the NFL and a standing tee time with your foursome might meet that need. But for those of you who do especially derive comfort from participating in religious rituals, the good news is that some Buddhist traditions meet the "old-time religion" requirement that many people seem to need in order to feel like they're a part of something bigger. In the Buddhist world you can "go to church" every day if you like, and on the full moon of every month there is a religious holiday to celebrate.

If you really want to worship something, my mentors suggested worshipping trees. Trees are living beings, and they are our brothers and sisters who do so much good for us. In some real sense, the Buddha worshipped the tree under which he gained enlightenment. "If you want to worship your creator," they added, "then worship your parents."

"Good answer," I thought.

If you're a Judeo-Christian kind of guy, you might think that embracing the Buddha's wisdom constitutes a negation of your present beliefs. Does studying the Dharma and following the Buddhist path actually make you a traitor to your religion? Well, the Buddha never took a stand on whether there's a central intelligence in command of the universe—a God, so to speak, with a capital G—because, he said, he wasn't concerned about that. But you have to look at that statement in context. As a dude and not a god, he couldn't claim to know anything more about metaphysical stuff than anybody else. The Buddha also said that everything should be questioned, including what he himself said. That's because, to quote an old country-and-western song, "You've got to walk that lonesome valley / You've got to walk it by yourself / Oh, nobody else can walk it for you..."

Nowhere in the Buddhist world did people impose the Buddha's philosophy on other people, and those who spread the Dharma throughout Asia tended to respect the deities and beliefs of those to whom they preached. Buddha's take on religion is that if the religion teaches peace and compassion, then by all means follow it. If it teaches hatred, then (as they say in Jersey) "Fuhgeddaboudit."

You're responsible for your own life. *You* have to make good choices and obtain wisdom on your own. And you can only gain real wisdom through *personal experience*. If you put your faith in what others say instead of what you have learned for yourself, then you're a patsy.

So here's my take on the whole can-a-Christian-be-a-Buddhist issue. There is nothing about Buddhism in its most essential form that contradicts anything espoused by any other religion. The idea that Buddhism is an "atheistic religion" doesn't stem from some "There is no God" core belief. Buddhism just doesn't go there. Studying the Dharma is about gaining wisdom about how to get the most out of your life, about Being All That You Can Be. You can be Christian or Jewish and Buddhist at the same time. Lots of people are. Just bear in mind that Buddhism recommends skepticism about anything that other people tell you is true. If God has touched your life in some way, that's proof enough of His existence because it comes from your personal experience.

I have even heard Jesus referred to by Buddhists. Some monks I've met believe that during his missing years between his Bar Mitzvah and the beginning of his ministry, the juvenile Jesus traveled to northern India and the Himalayas and studied with Buddhist monks. When you think about it, Jesus's words and Gautama's recommendations bear some very strong similarities. Whether it's true that Jesus was influenced by Buddhism or not, the two traditions share a good deal in common when it comes to the value of kindness and compassion for our fellow man.

Wherever the Dharma spread, proselytizers didn't encourage the local population to get rid of whatever deities they already worshipped. In many Sri Lankan homes today, for example, people will bracket their Buddha image with those of Hindu "household" gods. Some people even hang hideous masks in the parlor to scare away demons, even though Buddhism doesn't officially swing that way at all.

Buddha discouraged superstition.

4
So, Like, What Is Truth?

At the heart of what the Buddha taught lies the idea that there are truths that, when we really understand them, entirely change our lives. The Buddha said that there are four such truths, which he called the Four Noble Truths. These four truths are very simple:

- The First Noble Truth is that life consists of suffering.
- The Second Noble Truth is that suffering is caused by something.
- The Third Noble Truth is that suffering can be stopped.
- The Fourth Noble Truth is that there is a particular way to make the suffering stop.

For all beings, human or otherwise, life kinda sucks. The First Noble Truth reminds us that we are born in pain, live in misery, and die, as Woody Allen said, much too soon. The good stuff is fleeting and impermanent (think orgasm, here, for instance). All the great events and experiences in our lives are like orgasms. They're here, they're wonderful, and then they're gone. Einstein once explained relativity this way: "Put your hand on a hot stove for a minute, and it seems like an hour. Sit with a pretty girl for an hour, and it seems like a minute." In life, it seems like we spend more time with our hands on hot stoves than we do with pretty girls.

Bummed out yet? Just remember, there's a light at the end of the tunnel.

The Second Noble Truth answers the question *what causes suffering?* It doesn't just cover the obvious stuff, like getting old or getting sick and dying, being rejected by a lover or getting run over by a drunk driver. Buddhism doesn't explain what doesn't need to be explained. But sometimes we experience suffering and we don't even realize it.

In reality even the good stuff causes suffering. For all the pleasures we take in alcohol, drugs, chocolate cake, cheeseburgers, big suburban houses with lawns, sunny days, and sport utility vehicles, there are also hangovers, addictions, thunder thighs, arteriosclerosis, urban blight, skin cancer, and global warming. Sex? Personally, I love sex. The pleasure cortex inside my brain is shaped like the Playboy Bunny. Nevertheless, the list of miseries and disasters sex can generate is endless.

Wanting itself is unhappiness, and unhappiness is suffering. The cause of misery is the desire to satisfy oneself without ever being able to. You can't have your cake and eat it, too. As much as you want a new car, you only have a new car for a few days. Depreciation kicks in the minute you drive it off the lot, and the second you're on the road, that Camry is already on its way to the junkyard. *Contentment* is happiness. Happiness

is a dependable used car. How many Lexus owners worry about their finish being scratched by
some punk with a handful of keys? If you're
driving a muddy '97 Dodge pickup, getting keyed
probably isn't a blip on your worry radar.

Of course you will always want things, but
an unwholesome attachment to something is
what the Buddha called "craving" or "clinging."
Craving is a big cause of suffering. Let's get real
here. You know people who define themselves
by what they own. Are they truly happy people?
Or do their lives seem full of stuff yet empty otherwise? Do trophy wives and 8,000-square-foot
houses with half a dozen bathrooms lead to contentment? We know that people who have so
much often want more. In the end, do we have
to look much past our own culture to see how
destructive greed can be?

One night while watching the *Late Show
with David Letterman* I heard a story about
Frank Sinatra that made perfect Buddhist sense.
Shaking hands and greeting a long line of fans,

As much as you want a new car, you only have
a new car for a few days.

Sinatra was observed interacting with a man who admired Frank's diamond cufflinks. Sinatra said, "You want them?" and right then and there he began taking them off.

The fan put up his hands and said, "Oh, no, Mr. Sinatra. I don't want them. I was just admiring them."

But Sinatra took them off anyway, and he pressed them into the grateful fan's hands. A comedian who frequently opened for Sinatra said to him, "I can't believe you did that, Frank. Those were thousand dollar cufflinks!" (And those were 1960 dollars!) To his surprise Sinatra just replied, "If you own something you can't bear to part with, you don't own it, it owns you."

It is natural to want things, but you can't let wanting or craving control you. Take Nookie. How many marriages end because the husband wants to have sex with someone hotter and more exciting than the woman who gave him children? I think it's tragic when that happens.

"If you own something you can't bear to part with,
you don't own it, it owns you."

Good grief, dude. Draw yourself a pencil-thin mustache with her eyebrow pencil, make a dramatic entrance into the bedroom, and introduce yourself as "Raooooul." Esperanza awaits.

You don't have to be poor to be Buddhist. But Buddhism also does not teach that poverty is an obstacle to happiness. Even in our own culture, corrupt executives and greedy corporate leeches are counterbalanced by wealthy and generous philanthropists. Jesus said it was harder for a camel to pass through the eye of a needle than for a rich man to enter heaven. But he didn't say it was impossible, did he? Similarly, the Buddhists believe that there is nothing wrong with being rich, so long as you don't hurt anyone. It is even better if you do good, meritorious things and are generous with your wealth.

In order to attain real happiness in life, you have to know where happiness comes from. The Second Noble Truth, the truth about what causes suffering, tells you where *not* to look. If you go looking for happiness in the wrong places, your want and craving will overwhelm whatever conventional happiness you derive from buying, consuming, or making love.

The Third Noble Truth, the truth that suffering has an end, tells us that we don't have to suffer. I know a monk from Sri Lanka who, when he was ten years old, watched helplessly as the authorities arrested his three older brothers and took them away in handcuffs and blindfolds, never to be seen again. After this same boy took refuge at a nearby monastery, a man who was carrying a baby sought safety there. That man was shot dead at the boy's feet trying to escape the police.

Let's face facts. If you're lucky enough to have escaped tragedy in your life thus far, the only thing that could prevent you from experiencing grief in the future would be your own instantaneous death. Grief is an inevitable, universal cause of suffering, and the pain it causes can last for a long time. No one can avoid grief. I would be surprised if I found that even the holiest man in Buddhism was not affected by the death of a loved one. Even animals grieve.

Obtaining the kind of inner strength and objectivity you need to transcend something as natural as grief is difficult. Buddhists have a word for it: *enlightenment*. But grief isn't the only kind of suffering, is it? Let's see, there's physical pain, illness, desire, craving, aversion, anger, depression, worry, getting old, being victimized, erectile dysfunction, disappointment, anger, lust, dead car batteries...

Transcending these things doesn't mean that you're not going to experience them. Instead, Buddhism tells you how to deal with them so you can minimize their impact on your life. You can, in fact, rid yourself of melancholy, worry, lust, and anger. Although you can't eliminate grief altogether, you can learn to handle it along with pain, disease, and aging, by cultivating your own inner strength. You are the master of your fate; you are the architect of your own salvation. You have to develop these resources within yourself, and Buddhism shows just how to do that. When you do so, you don't just overcome the things in life that suck, you attain happiness. Real happiness, genuine happiness. The thing we're all really looking for, our whole lives long.

5
The Middle Path

The Fourth Noble Truth, the truth that there is a way to make the suffering stop, shows us the way to happiness. It's a little involved, so bear with me. There are a few *thou shalt nots* involved, but in Buddhism the don'ts are secondary to the dos—the positive steps you take to make yourself happy, content, and immune to suffering. Let's deal with the no-nos first and get them out of the way.

The Buddhist version of the Ten Commandments is called the Five Precepts. The Five Precepts are directives against killing, stealing, sexual misconduct, lying, and taking intoxicants.

Buddha and the great Christian writer C. S. Lewis both refer to something called "natural law"—a type of "law" that we should not confuse with the laws of nature and that has nothing to do with big fish eating little fish. Natural law is something deep inside the consciousness of decent people that tells them, no matter what culture or historical era they live in, that there are things which are just plain wrong for people to do. Murdering your neighbor, raping his wife, stealing his single malt Scotch, and then telling the police you were in Montreal the whole time is not civilized behavior. Written prohibitions against these things date all the way back to Hammurabi and Moses, a long time before the Buddha came around. No doubt these were issues in prehistoric times, too.

When we say, "Don't do it to me and I won't do it to you," we articulate a building block for civilization. This idea is common among humankind, but it's still subject to interpretation. In other words, different cultures express the idea differently, and Buddhism, too, offers its own unique elaboration on it. Let's take the First Precept, for example:

Killing—don't do it.

People have debated the precise terms of "Thou shalt not kill" since God first committed the words to tablet over four millennia ago. Ancient Hebrews still warred against squatters in the Holy Land, and today most countries in the Middle East seem to take the rule with a grain of salt. "Thou shalt not kill" didn't seem to slow the Christians down much during the Crusades and the Inquisition, nor did it stop people from fighting in Kosovo in the late '90s. But, in principle, every decent person knows that killing another person is wrong, regardless of the justifications that governments might give for executing someone.

Buddhists tend to take the "no killing" rule even more seriously than Judeo-Christian cultures, extending the prohibition on killing to all living things, human or otherwise. Buddhists essentially have a "no exception" clause in their beliefs when it comes to violence and the taking of life. If a Jew or a Christian or a Muslim or a Hindu can, in certain circumstances, make exceptions to rules about killing other beings, Buddhists, on the other hand, don't take kindly to the killing of anything that's alive, be it a suicide bomber or a spider.

True, circumstances sometimes call for self-defense. (We're Buddhist, after all, not stupid.) If a guy's coming at me intending to brain me with a baseball bat, I'm going to try to stop him with any means at my disposal. The holiest man on the mountaintop would do the same. But war, for any reason whatsoever, is a no-no. No war, no exceptions. This is why we don't tend to see wars fought in the name of the Buddha.

The paradoxes that different beliefs can present are interesting. People who believe in Creation, for example, also believe that God doesn't make mistakes. As a consequence of this belief, they must admit that leeches, ticks, and mosquitoes are all God's creatures, put here for a purpose. That doesn't stop Creation-believers from killing them or anything else put here under man's dominion if it's in man's best interests. Buddhists also see leeches, ticks, and mosquitoes as pests, and since a big part of the Buddhist world is malaria country, mosquitoes can be villains of the worst sort. Even so, Buddhists believe it's wrong to kill a mosquito. Or a cow. Or a Christian. If you make an exception for mosquitoes, then you're leaving the rule open for interpretation, and misinterpretation. Everything that's alive wants to stay alive, just like us humans.

But again, the Dharma does not override common sense. Just as in situations of self-defense (I know some monks in Asia who could go all Shaolin on someone who needs it), controlling mosquito populations saves human lives by the millions every year. Malaria is the world's number one people killer. Can we cast aspersions on the pork processing plant over our link sausages and waffles? But even in cases of self-defense, Buddhists know that the most important thing here is not hating other beings, even ones who are trying to do you harm.

Although one's intentions have a lot to do with rendering the swamp disease free of malarial parasites, or taking out the rabid dog that's about to bite your daughter, it's still killing, and killing has consequences: each time you kill something, it makes it easier to kill the next thing. So refraining from taking life to the best of one's ability requires mindfulness and good judgment. I've never killed a spider in my life. I've always thought it was much more entertaining to catch them and let them go outside, or to cohabitate with them. There is no critter more purely beneficial to humankind than spiders. If you take the Don't Kill a Spider pledge, you can improve your karma and cure yourself of the willies at the same time.

The Second Precept tells us that we shouldn't steal:

> *Don't take anything that doesn't*
> *belong to you without permission.*

That's a pretty basic rule, and outside the world of macroeconomics, there is not much to interpret here. Some societies amputate the hands of people who are found guilty of stealing. Kids used to get paddled in school for stealing. Prisons are full of thieves. So, just as we naturally know that we shouldn't kill, it seems universally accepted that we shouldn't steal as well. The Buddhist spin on the taboo against theft is that stealing things when you already have what you need indicates excessive craving, the primary cause of suffering. It also makes you a total jerk.

The Third Precept concerns sex:

Do not misconduct yourself sexually.

Note that it doesn't say that you can't fool around. If you choose to become a monk, that's a different story. Laypeople, however, are encouraged to marry and are allowed to have all the sex they can stand. Marriage seems to be one of those "natural" laws, one that's built in to the human psyche. There has never been a society or culture on earth that didn't have marriage.

While we're on the subject of marriage, I want to share with you the funniest joke I've ever heard:

Back in the day when people traveled mostly by train, an overnighter was overbooked, and the conductor asked a man and a woman who didn't know each other to share a sleeping compartment. He reminded them that because it was wartime, sacrifices had to be made. They agreed, and the man took the top bunk, the woman the lower one. Everything was fine until about two in the morning, when the man felt the woman poking him from below with her feet.

"What is it?" the man asked.

"I'm cold," the woman said, and a little coquettishly she asked, "Would you go get me a blanket?"

The man thought a second. "I've got a better idea," he said. "Why don't we pretend we're man and wife?"

The woman thought it over, giggled, and then said, "OK."

"Good," said the man. "Go get your own damn blanket."

In the traditional Buddhist world, sex is fine, so long as it happens between husband and wife. (And like everyone everywhere else, Buddhists have their share of marital problems.) But does the Third Precept, which only mentions "sexual misconduct," allow for more or less room for interpretation than, say, "Thou shalt not commit adultery?" Well, adultery is certainly sexual misconduct. As with the rest of the precepts, not harming others is a major consideration here. When you've promised another person that you'll be faithful to them and treat them with respect, it's certainly hurtful to turn around and cheat on them.

What about gay sex? Well, in an important way, this precept is about sex in a committed relationship, regardless of the genders of the people in it. Again, a healthy committed partnership is commended. Gay sex may be discouraged by certain societies in which Buddhism has found itself, but the Buddha himself wasn't interested in reproaching anyone as long as they did right by others. I have gay Buddhist friends in the military. That should not surprise anyone.

How many good relationships—even if they are not sanctioned by marital vows—are healthier and more legitimate than sad, loveless, and codependent marriages? Intention carries a lot of weight in Buddhism. Compare the relative merits of a hot live-in love affair between two college students who adore each other to a twenty-year loveless marriage between a mousy, depressed mother of four and an abusive slob? When it's an expression of mutual love, sex is a beautiful thing. But if one person coerces and bullies the other into having sex, it's something else entirely.

There is a famous story in Asia about two monks, an elderly one and a young one, who are walking down a forest path, and they come upon

"Good," said the man.
"Go get your own damn blanket."

a river—wade-able, but challenging. There on the bank sat an old, frail woman, and she asked the monks if they could help her cross the river.

Now in their tradition, monks never touch or are touched by women. Even when they talk to each other they stay pretty far apart. But the elder monk told the old woman to climb upon his back, and he "piggy-backed" her across the stream, set her down on the opposite bank, and the two monks proceeded on their way.

After a little ways, the young monk was about to burst from indignation. "I can't believe you did that!" he scolded the old monk. "You've been a monk for fifty years, and you have never broken a precept. And just now, you threw it all away!"

The old monk replied: "I put the woman down after we crossed the river. It is you who is still carrying her."

The Fourth Precept doesn't mince words:

Don't lie.

The Buddha doesn't beat this issue to death, mainly because Buddhism is so focused on truth and the power that comes with truth. Certainly honesty presents its own challenges. But it's an honest person's karma that people will trust him; he might not get elected to high office, but he'll be believed.

Actually, telling the truth is the easy part. You've actually also got to take into consideration how and when you do it. Buddhists aim to tell the truth affectionately, at the right time, and beneficially. If you do those things, you don't need to be too concerned about how the truth affects others—that's their problem. If someone has problems with the truth, it's because the truth tends to unsettle his comfortable world obscured by delusion. This is the world Buddhism works to free us from. Mind that there is a difference between real, freeing truth and our sanctimonious opinions. And another thing: there is a "middle path" between telling lies and telling the truth. People should take it more seriously. It's called shutting up and listening.

The Fifth Precept is a groaner for American and British dudes:

Avoid intoxicants.

That one sounds a bit rigid for a body of philosophy aimed at avoiding extremes. Does this mean that a person who is in pain shouldn't take morphine? Of course not. Part of what refraining from intoxicants is about is the personal and social costs of addiction. Addiction, like adultery, ruins people's lives—it causes harm to oneself and others. The taboo against intoxicants is also meant to safeguard the other four precepts, the logic being that one would be more likely to kill, steal, lie, or commit sexual misconduct under the influence of intoxicants. This makes perfect sense. Stories of people doing things that they deeply regret while they were drunk are everywhere. I have a few myself.

The vast majority of people who drink don't have a drinking problem, but like all the precepts, the wording of this one makes it sound absolute. But the principle of the precept, as with all the others, is to consciously refrain from causing harm to others. Me? I drink. But I don't drink to the point of losing self-discipline, or even getting the giggles. I'm not a drunk, and I don't ever get drunk. I do drink exactly one drink every day, though. Under some circumstances, like when my wife has a night off from her third-shift job as a nurse, I may exceed the one-drink rule and split a bottle of chianti or pinot noir with her. I've also been known to break the first and the last of the Five Precepts simultaneously when I bring beer along on a fishing trip.

When the monks thought that I knew enough about Buddhism to teach it back in the States, I was asked: do you keep the precepts? I admitted that I broke two. Number one, I drink alcohol, but never more than two drinks a day, usually one, and sometimes none.

"Then you are keeping the precept," the monk said. "In America, that counts as not drinking."

Then he asked me what other precept I break. I admitted that I break the First Precept, in that I like to catch fish. And eat them.

The monk bristled. "You need a new hobby!" he declared.

Nevertheless, I remain confidently Buddhist. Warm beer on a cold day near an ice-cold stream. I'm not there to catch trout. I'm there to bliss out on the sights, sounds, smells, skin sensations, and tastes of standing hip deep in moving water on an otherwise cheerless, cloudy day, watching my homemade dry fly sink like a pebble in a deep upstream pool. The Buddha loved the outdoors, too. The more beautiful the place, and the more developed your Buddhist sensibilities, the more intoxicating the experience is.

"You've been a monk for fifty years,
and you have never broken a precept.
And just now, you threw it all away!"

When I chose to follow the Middle Path, I knew very well that, even though traditional Buddhism is short on the metaphysical, there still would be aspects of the belief system I would find hard to swallow. One was rebirth, which I've come to grips with, even though I'd really rather believe that it isn't true in a certain literal sense. Samsara, the ceaseless cycle of birth-death-rebirth, isn't about fun; it's about suffering. Over and over again, until you can rid yourself completely of the thing that causes suffering.

The other is karma.

What is karma? Translated literally, karma means "action," and it basically refers to actions-and-their-consequences—but it does not have anything to do with, as many people suppose, the rewards or punishments people reap as a result of their actions. Karma can be understood simply through cause-and-effect. Smile at a child, the child smiles back. Kiss your wife on the back of her neck while she's at the sink, and you get a purr and a twerk. Tickle a baby, and she giggles and wiggles. Yell at your dog for running away, he runs farther away. Get good grades in school and you get into college. Get too drunk and obnoxious and say the wrong thing, and somebody might kick your ass.

I analogize karma this way: if you're an appliance repairman, you are more likely to retire comfortably than a murdering, thieving thug. But that doesn't mean that life somehow guarantees that a murdering, thieving thug won't kill you on your way home from your retirement party. Bad things still happen to good people, and there's no use trying to figure out why—it's kind of just crappy luck. Let's get real here. Buddhism is a "how-to" ethic for living a good life, not a way to put the Whammy on anybody.

Karma does have its metaphysical aspects, however. I will point out that Buddhist metaphysical beliefs, like Christian ones, include both a heaven and a hell.

The heaven versus rebirth issue is a complicated one that I'll avoid speculating about. I'm as clueless as the next guy about the reality of either option, and like everyone else, I'll just have to take whatever the end of life dishes out. However, regarding rebirth in a heaven or a hell, Buddhism says you won't be stuck in either realm for eternity. You might not get to stay in heaven forever, but the good news is that even people who land in hell have a chance to work their way out.

I guess what karma boils down to is that your volitional actions impact your present life and factor into whatever happens when it ends. If life continues past what we define as death, then karma helps determine the nature of that continued life. If you live virtuously, good things happen. You might not reap rewards right away, but rest assured that positive actions have positive effects.

One day when I was living at the Sri Bodhiraja Monastery, the chief priest summoned me to his office, which was in a small clay hut—the coolest place on campus.

Bhante Sobhita was expecting a visitor in a few days. It was a white woman from New Zealand who became a bhikkhuni—a Buddhist nun. She was coming to ask him a specific question: How do Buddhists deal with the issue of free will? He wasn't familiar with the term, especially in its religious context, so he wanted to ask me about it.

I told him that to understand free will he needed to know its opposite, predestination. I told him that some Christians believe that God predetermines everyone's fate, and that people can do nothing to change it. Free will, I told him, is the idea that each man has the power to determine his own fate.

The monk's usual scowl deepened, and he considered what I told him. Finally, he said, "But both are untrue. Everything is connected to everything else."

This is what I like about Buddhism: it's simple.

Most of humankind cannot bear the notion that some essence of them does not persist after death. For the life of me, I don't know why. What's so bad about ceasing to exist? Do I want to be *me* for the rest of eternity, even if I wind up in heaven? Then again, I'm not sure I can bear the notion of being reborn—of hitting the "reset" button for another life of suffering and misery.

Many people use the term "reincarnation" where I would say "rebirth." There is a difference between these two ideas. Reincarnation might be something along the lines of General George Patton's belief that he returned again and again as warriors in the great battles of history. Rebirth is the result of ignorance of the way to avoid it.

There are many stories that indicate that rebirth is real, but things have also happened in my own life, particularly in my Buddhist life, that seem strongly to suggest that the force of actions in past lives does exist. In 2002, when I went to Sri Lanka, my original destination was Pakistan, and in 2003, when I went to Sri Lanka again, my original destination had been China. But between the Taliban, SARS, and opportunity, I ended up immersed in the Buddhist world for six months, landing at the feet of three of the most eminent theologians in the country. It was like I was meant to be a Buddhist.

Go figure.

We could speculate until the cows come home about whether or not life continues after death, or about how rebirth is possible. But I think it would be more useful here to share with you something I wrote for a family when they requested a Buddhist funeral service for their loved one.

My Vietnamese monk friend Venerable Thich Hang Dat called me and asked if I could help him with a funeral, for a guy named Fred. I said, "Absolutely." I would do anything that man asked. He's the best monk I've ever known.

I went along with Master Hang Dat for the last visit to the family in Southern Indiana. I think he invited me so that the family would have a regular American Buddhist to talk to as well as a Vietnamese monk. I saw Fred from his bedside, in a coma, snoring away. Twenty-four hours later, Fred was gone.

At the funeral Master Hang Dat took the podium and delivered a short, brutal-feeling eulogy about how humans turn into garbage when they die. Then he led the Vietnamese contingent in a series of long chants. They gave him a good send-off.

I knew many of the Vietnamese contingent from the temple we attended: successful business people, many of them, who took off working hours to go to the funeral of a white man they didn't even know. The core of Buddhism worldwide is made up of people like them, people who put the needs of others before their own, even for dead strangers. Compassion is everything.

At Venerable Thich Hang Dat's bidding I prepared a little handout called "Buddhism's Perspective on Death" for the people who would attend Fred's funeral. With ssome small changes, this is what it said:

> In the Buddhist way of thinking, a person's death is not the end of existence. We can all sense the life energy within us, and we cannot imagine that this does not endure, somehow. We love life and cling fervently to it, and when a loved one is very sick and dying, we yearn for a way to prolong that person's life, no matter how much that person suffers, because we know their loss will leave us lonely, or maybe even alone.
>
> We know that life, like everything else in the universe, will fall just as surely as it has risen. Impermanence is the one constant thing we can expect. People die, but so do stars and galaxies. Still,

the matter and the energy of an exploding star do not cease to exist, but rather assume different forms. This is important to remember: nothing is lost when someone dies.

Buddhists believe in rebirth. When this body and mind dies, the body and mind of something or someone new is born somewhere else. We don't take our identities with us—identity is as changing as the tides. However, as all the major religions believe, our actions now determine what happens later. Buddhists call this karma. From the Buddhist perspective you might not have to die and go to heaven to re-encounter your beloved grandparent.

Nothing is lost when someone dies. The nature of impermanence is not obliteration; the nature of impermanence is change. When we prepare ourselves wisely for decay, aging, sickness,

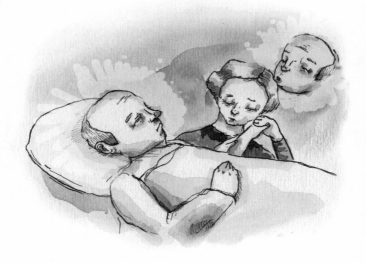

Humans can free themselves from such suffering by
loving wisely and with understanding, and with the
constant reminder that nothing lasts forever.

and death, they will not be as difficult to bear. The reality of even our own death must be measured against the death of every person who has ever lived. And it may very well be that it is ourselves who live and die, over and over again.

Why? People suffer, after all, all their lives.

It's love. Love is the reason, and the attachments and clinging that are the results of love. Buddhists believe that eternal bliss comes only to people who are completely free from desire and attachment. It will take us many lifetimes to get there. So in a sense, we are condemned to love. A Buddhist will take advantage of this by loving everyone, and will reap the benefit of true happiness on earth, which comes from living a moral, selfless, and especially a compassionate life.

But as the Buddha has warned us, love

that turns into unhealthy attachment is the root of all suffering. Humans can free themselves from such suffering by loving wisely and with understanding, and with the constant reminder that nothing lasts forever.

How It's Done for Real

The Buddhist guide to successful living is called the Noble Eightfold Path. It's the blueprint for a proper life, humankind's user's manual. It's what you're *supposed* to do. All eight list out as follows:

1. Right Understanding	Wisdom
2. Right Thought	
3. Right Speech	Ethical Conduct
4. Right Action	
5. Right Livelihood	
6. Right Effort	Mental Discipline
7. Right Mindfulness	
8. Right Concentration	

These eight notions constitute the Fourth Noble Truth, the truth of the path that leads to the end of suffering. The eight can be grouped into three categories based on the type of practice they embody: some are practices of *ethical conduct*, others involve *mental discipline*, and others are meant to cultivate *wisdom*. If we intend to lead the best possible lives, then we must work at all of these things. As should be becoming evident, the essence of all of these practices and the source of true happiness can be boiled down to wisdom and compassion. *Compassion.* Hang on to that word. It's the most important word in Buddhism.

You should keep in mind that you don't cultivate the path within yourself one part at a time; you have to learn to develop these skills concurrently. For now let's skip over the first two categories of the Noble Path (we'll return to them later) and get into the three action-oriented topics: Right Speech, Right Action, and Right Livelihood.

Right Speech implies thoughtfulness with

regard to the words that come out of your mouth. Not lying is an important part of Right Speech, but Buddhists also refrain from gossip, backbiting, rudeness, harshness, and saying abusive things. You also have to avoid bullshit—idle, time-wasting chatter. Be polite and friendly, gentle, meaningful, constructive, and encouraging. Say things that are true, useful, and beneficial. Say it nicely, or don't say it at all.

My dog Trixie has run off from us on occasion. Once when it happened, my wife bellowed: "Trixie! Bad dog! Get over here." And of course she didn't obey; who in doggie-land would come to someone using that tone of voice? I whistled and called out "Trixie, come!" the sweetest way I could and patted my thighs like I wanted to play. Trixie trotted right up to me with a smile on her face. And the light bulb went on over my wife's head.

Right Action invites us to live a life that is honorable, compassionate, peaceful, and moral. This is accomplished, unsurprisingly, by doing honorable, compassionate, peaceful, and moral things.

In this sense, Right Action is a positive expression of the "don'ts" listed in the Five Precepts.

I love a positive spin. "Don't commit adultery" sounds pretty sleazy, doesn't it? I'm surprised it's not followed by, "And while you're at it, keep your hands out of your pockets." You know what sounds better? "I love my wife. And because I love her, I am faithful to her." The positive makes the admonition unnecessary. I'm not walking around grumbling because I'm forbidden to go to the Happy Endings Massage Parlor; I'm happy because I am in love. (Plus I think she's still pretty hot stuff, too, after forty years.) Right Action is about what you do, not what you don't do. Love, after all, is a dimension of compassion, and compassion makes us happy.

Then there's *Right Livelihood*. People have to make a living, after all. In Buddhist life, what you do and don't do to earn your daily bread is important. Apart from telling his business-minded followers not to cheat people, the Buddha offered examples of shady dealings that we can translate into contemporary terms: dealing in arms, poisons, intoxicants, or human flesh—really any job that requires or facilitates killing or exploitation—is suspect. There were no Enrons in Buddha's day, no corporate polluters or rocket-propelled grenades, no crack cocaine, nuclear proliferation, international sex slavery, or insider trading. But there were butchers, pimps, hired thugs, and usurers. It's not as if the Buddha was unfamiliar with the darker side of commerce.

Right Livelihood doesn't mean that everyone should become a doctor, teacher, nurse, or social worker. People do business because that's what people do, and there is no reason for altruists to be smug about the good they accomplish through their work. The richest people in the world contribute millions of dollars to good causes, and if it is their forte to make money instead of running soup kitchens, then they're using their talents for good the best way they can. Charity, after all, is a dimension of compassion. Ask Bill and Melinda Gates.

For the ways in which they contribute to the betterment of society, I think that artists, storytellers, athletes, and entertainers are some of the world's most underrated people. Comparing Mother Teresa to Keith Richards might be the ultimate apples-and-oranges thing, but imagine what life would be like without art. Or college basketball, for that matter. Life without art or March Madness would be unbearable. Ballerinas, I believe, are just as important as brain surgeons. But doctors, for their part, might be more Buddhist than they realize. The only part of the Hippocratic Oath I know by heart are the first four words: First, do no harm.

That's the way the Dharma, particularly the practice of ethical conduct, looks at the world in general.

8
A Beautiful Mind

Now let's back up to consider the two wisdom-oriented items of the Noble Eightfold Path: Right Understanding and Right Thought.

Right Understanding involves perceiving the world without preconceptions, prejudices, ideological filters, conventional "wisdom," or bullshit. Truly seeing the world with wisdom helps you realize that *everything changes* and everything is *interconnected*. You are just a part of this grand concoction called your community. You are not an insular, unchanging creature with an identity so much as you are an ingredient in the universal gumbo. By understanding reality this way, in its "ultimate" form, you go past mere knowledge into the realm of what the Buddhists call *penetration*.

Mind out of the gutter, dudes. It's hard to describe what penetration is, other than to say that it's the ability to really, really, really, really wrap your head around something.

Buddhists are seriously into the development of the mind. People strongly associate Buddhist practice with meditation, and for good reason, though of course all religions have meditative aspects and practices. Buddhist meditation is widely misunderstood, so I will elaborate on it in detail when we get to the final items of the path. But as we discuss wisdom, which comes as the result of mental discipline, it is important to realize that meditation *develops* awareness rather than shuts it down. Meditators aren't supposed to zone out; they're supposed to tune in.

Penetration is developed through meditation. It involves peering into your own mind and growing to truly understand yourself. Through meditation you shuffle off the preconceived notions (read "mental blocks") that present barriers to unvarnished understanding. By gaining such insight into yourself, you're able to interpret the world in fresh, new ways. The result is the greatest paradox in Buddhism. By coming to realize that impermanence is the immutable rule and that you are nothing, really, but what you've made of yourself in your mind, you achieve a personal freedom. This freedom is expressed through self-actualization, effectiveness, happiness, contentment, awareness, and compassion.

Right Thought is what you need to pull all this together. The ability to see the world naked, so to speak, then turns you into someone who sheds selfish desire, ill will, thoughts of violence and evil, hatred, and anger. Why? Because they're foolish wastes of time, that's why. These thoughts and feelings are harmful and destructive to you and to others. The people who do most of the conspicuous overconsumption, hate-mongering, and violence-generating do so not so much because they're evil but because they don't know the truth. They don't get that the big deal they're making about themselves or their issues don't amount to Shinola in the long run. They lack wisdom. They suffer from ignorance. That's right, they're morons.

Surprisingly, feelings of compassion, love, and magnanimity fill the vacuum where your delusions used to be. When you first "get it," you might experience frustration, like you know a secret that most other people don't, even though you wish they did. Overall, though, you'll feel a renewed sense of faith in humanity. Why? Because you come to realize that there are people who've never read a word of the Dharma who are the most peace-making, unspoiled, guileless, generous, and beneficial people on earth. There are swarms of wonderful people around who are basically Buddhists and don't even know it.

But Right Thought doesn't turn you into Rebecca of Sunnybrook Farm. On the contrary, Right Thought is inspired by the world as it is—

warts, unpleasant people, dubious leadership, and all. Right Thought leads to Right Action. Take death, for instance: If you can perceive your demise as a natural part of the human condition, a part about which you can do nothing other than to respond to it when it is imminent, you will be able to die well and support those who will suffer when you die. Who wants to be around a brooding, bitter person? Dying is no excuse to be an asshole.

Can you see how all of these aspects of the Noble Eightfold Path tie together? Your development along the Path is not sequential. All eight dimensions develop simultaneously. Right Thought is derived from Right Understanding and results in Right Action. Right Understanding comes from mental discipline, the topic of the last three elements of the Eightfold Path. But you're not likely to take up that development without a rudimentary understanding of the knowledge that changes your perspective, i.e., the Dharma.

Much has been written about the phenomenon of paradigm shift, a thing that happens when you radically change your outlook on things based on new information, like a pacifist after Pearl Harbor or a faith healer with appendicitis. As a result of a paradigm shift, your behavior also changes. Practicing Buddhism basically paves the way for a paradigm shift on a gigantic scale.

Right Understanding carries along with it some pretty heavy baggage. It's hard to look at yourself with total honesty, to see that you have deluded yourself about many aspects of your life, and then winnow out your own self-delusions and dispense with them. This process can be downright painful, like giving birth to your new self. But through this effort you end up liking yourself a whole lot more than you used to.

There is a great chasm between Right Understanding and Right Thought. How do we go from realizing that we are of little consequence to becoming people motivated by compassion? Consider how easy it is to become angry: because anger is a visceral, instinctual reaction, we often get angry without even thinking about it. We only grow to be able to deal effectively with anger by cultivating mental discipline over time. We have to work at it. It's the same with compassion. Only through mental discipline can we grow to become people motivated by wise and compassionate thoughts.

9
The Well-Trained Brain

When we are ignorant about the bigger picture, we may try to find happiness by giving in to cravings and desires. But once we see how things really are, we recognize that true happiness is only achieved through acts of love, generosity, and compassion. We start to understand that this is the key to finding real happiness. Right Understanding enables us to realize that this is the way, and Right Thought and Right Action allow us to make it a reality. But if we don't make an effort to discipline our minds, we won't be able to pull off the transformation of thought and action needed to experience the full measure of human happiness. We're talking about happiness most people can barely imagine. We're talking bliss here.

So now we can turn our attention to the mental discipline-oriented aspects of the Noble Eightfold Path: Right Effort, Right Mindfulness, and Right Concentration.

Stop what you're doing, right now. (I hope you're not operating heavy machinery.) Sit as still as you possibly can. Pretend that you're a Marine, all alone in a forward listening post at night. You're scared, your senses are heightened, and you feel like you have Superman hearing. You can even feel vibration through your skin. A human motion detector, you are keenly aware of everything around you—the coolness of the air, the rustling of the leaves, the faint noises of the guys behind the wire behind you, and the dead silence of the rough terrain ahead. Something moves close by, but you know it's just a lizard. Interesting: no flies buzzing around for once. You check one more time to see if there is a round chambered in your rifle, just to make sure.

This is what Buddhists call *Right Mindfulness*—a keen awareness of everything that's going on around you and inside of you. It's the exact opposite of wandering around with your head up your ass. It's the ultimate in living in the present, and it is something that Buddhist practitioners work hard to develop through meditation.

All right, back to the forward listening post, jarhead.

A sound so imperceptible—so quiet that you would never have heard it if you didn't have Superman hearing—echoes in the distance. The sound is so hushed and hesitant that the more you hear it, the more you're certain it's made by a human—a very professional, sneaky human. It takes forever, it seems, but the sound, just an occasional crumbling of dirt or a swish of fabric, gets closer. No animal out there moves like that. There are no big cats or other predators. It's a human, all right. You are so focused on that sound that after a while, you figure out that the human is moving diagonally toward your position. If he stays on the course he seems to be taking, he'll cross in front of you at maybe fifty meters. You sight down your rifle once more. *He's got to pass either in front of or behind that big gray rock...*

A twig snaps, and afterward there is absolute silence for a half-hour. But then, he's moving again. You know that if he passes on your side of the big gray rock, you'll see him, and you're afraid that he'll hear the pounding of your heart. Your hands are shaking, but your total focus is on that intermittent sound. *Real close now...*

Movement! There he is, crouching, moving one slow step at a time, and finally his form is silhouetted in front of the big gray rock. You take careful aim, center mass, and then you see him light a cigarette. In the nanosecond of light from the lighter, you can see clearly that he's one of your guys. You take your finger off the trigger, duck below the berm, and yell, "You stupid son of a bitch! I almost shot you!"

That nanosecond in which you recognize your buddy is the result of *Right Concentration*. Where Right Mindfulness can be described as a kind of hyper-awareness of everything that takes place around you, Right Concentration involves your ability to focus on the details.

Right Effort refers to the active, sustained practice of cultivating the mind. It takes real discipline to meditate. Sitting still and doing nothing can be truly difficult. It may even seem somehow un-American to sit still and do nothing. But you're not going to achieve anything meaningful until you do, well, *nothing*! Trust me when I say that the "doing nothing" of Buddhist meditation is the hardest nothing you'll ever do! You have to practice to be a practitioner of meditation. The bottom line is if you don't learn the proper way to do nothing, and you don't do nothing on a regular basis, you won't reap the full reward that all your hard-earned insight has to offer.

Your hands are shaking, but your total focus is on that
intermittent sound. Real close now...

10

Meditation: Can I Be a "Sorta-Kinda" Buddhist?

When you "get the point" and realize that developing your mind involves *tasks* and *processes* and *skill development*, you might think that you're faced with what appears to be sitting alone somewhere contemplating your navel. Nothing could be further from the truth. As still as you may be during a meditation session, you aren't supposed to zone out; you're supposed to be *aware*. Meditation is a discipline, and discipline takes effort. There are really two kinds of meditation: calming meditation and insight meditation, *shamatha* and *vipassana*. I've practiced calming meditation since the 1970s when I learned it from Transcendental Meditation, and

I gained a thorough understanding of it when I studied for four years with a Vietnamese Zen master, after I learned *vipassana* ("insight meditation") with the monks in Sri Lanka.

In order to penetrate into and investigate our minds and see things clearly, we've got to first quiet down our minds. Calming meditation helps us to focus our minds and weed out intrusive thoughts, and once we can concentrate we use analytical meditation to take a cold, hard look at things to see them for what they are.

When new practitioners try to meditate, even after proper instruction, they often become frustrated. The second your brain has "nothing" to do, we find out how difficult it really is to shut off the streaming jumble of thoughts that zing around inside our heads. Our "monkey mind," as it's affectionately called, distracts us, nags us, and irritates the crap out of us when we're trying to get some sleep. I've had serious monkey mind all my life. Staff Sergeant Dad frequently used to tell me to get my head out of my ass, which I took to mean, "Focus on what matters." He knew what he was talking about. An unfocused soldier soon becomes a dead soldier.

Thing is, focus takes work. Think of "meditation" like piano practice. The more you do it, the better you get at it. The better you get at it, the more your mind-monkeys start to quiet down. Eventually they even go away from time to time, and evicting them opens up space in your cranium. You attain a smidgen of wisdom from Dharma awareness and learn to see stuff a little more clearly, including yourself. Meditating will get easier and easier. Sitting there on that cushion you experience a sweet buzz. You can return to it every time you have a few minutes to spare, and life gets mellow indeed. You become the kind of guy who keeps his head when everyone else is losing theirs, and there's nothing cooler than that.

For those of you who just can't sit still, literally or figuratively, sitting cross-legged on a cushion with your eyes closed is not your only option.

Some traditional forms of meditation involve deliberate movement, usually walking. (Just don't try it at a busy intersection!) There are also ways to turn more or less rigorous activities into meditative endeavors. After a few easy lessons, you can run, hike, wash dishes, or rake leaves meditatively. If endurance isn't your thing, there are five-minute meditations. If it is, you can sign up for a two-week-long marathon session.

The most helpful kind of meditation is traditional sitting meditation. When you sit, the real magic happens. But there is nothing to be lost by turning a mundane activity, even one you might actually dread, into an exercise in which you learn to control your mind. Think of something like, say, taking a crap. Even the Buddha said that pooping can be meditative. My day always begins with ten minutes of sitting meditation with my jammy bottoms down around my ankles.

I am not a morning person, and as I age, the task of getting up out of bed is usually motivated by the pain I begin to feel after I've been lying down for a while. My "wakeup" meditation involves mindfulness of my physical self during the act of defecation. As I have practiced this meditation over the years, my pooping behaviors have changed. I am not in a hurry. I relax fully before I commence, unless of course there is some urgency to be expedient, and old copies of *American Angler* magazine do not distract me.

Once into the proper pooping frame of mind, I engage in "enlightened" pooping, which only involves just enough active participation (i.e., squeezing things out) to initiate peristalsis. Once you've very delicately induced launch sequence, then you totally relax again and meditate upon the sensation of your natural, unassisted evacuation. No straining or groaning. Your gut knows what it's supposed to do. You become a casual observer of your own crapping. Instead of thinking, "Geez, I wish I hadn't eaten all those jalapeños," you eventually train yourself to experience pooping as a sublime event. After that you're totally tuned in and ready to start the day.

Hobbies can be, and frequently are, meditations. I'm not saying that they have the same kind of sanity-inducing, soul-cleansing impact of traditional sitting meditation, but engaging in the right kinds of hobbies can be wonderful ways to meditate. We're talking about concentrative hobbies. My personal favorite is tying fishing flies. Bear in mind that it is impossible to think about two different things at the same time. Buddhism does not encourage multitasking. Knitting is only a meditation when you do it with the TV turned off. Reading and writing are not forms of meditation because the mind is too active while you're doing them. The jury's still out on listening to music. Some of it seems meditative, but most of it isn't. Mozart's good. I love music of all kinds, but I can't listen to music and do anything else at the same time but listen to the music, especially since I became a Buddhist.

For those of you who are inclined to pray to God, praying is meditation, especially when you shut up and let God do the talking. Singing or chanting can also be meditative. When you utter "The Lord is my Shepherd, I shall not want" or *Buddham sharanam gacchami* ("I take refuge in the Buddha," part of the traditional Buddhist prayer of refuge), you can aim beyond simply reciting what you've been taught.

You can take meditation lessons if you want to, but it's not really necessary. If you travel to Kandy, Sri Lanka, you can take an intensive course in vipassana meditation for free. TM (Transcendental Meditation) cost $200 when I took it in 1975, so that means it's probably two grand now. Personally I resent the significant part of the spiritual world that soaks seekers for every dollar they can get. I learned from the masters, and they didn't ask me for a single rupee the whole time I imposed on them. I'm not saying that there shouldn't be a fair exchange. I've done a lot of work for free for my gurus. But they weren't interested in selling Buddhism to me as a "therapeutic" thing. They were invested in my well-being for the sake of it. It's what they do.

My closest friend is a Sri Lankan monk named Nanda. We met at Sri Bodhiraja Temple in 2003, and in 2008 I brought him to America. I am twenty-five years older than he, but many times over the years I've gone to him for wisdom like he was my father. Other times, he's been my buddy. I take him to visit museums, and he gets me free food at a Thai restaurant whose owners feed him once a week. Nanda filled in the gaps for me when I left teaching sessions with the chief priest at Bodhiraja Temple with more questions than answers. He is both my "virtuous friend"—as Buddhists call our companions on walking the Middle Way—and my guru. When he lived in my house for a year I saw more of him than I did my wife.

He is not my only virtuous friend. When I met Greg he was a lieutenant on the Louisville police force. He is a veteran and a Buddhist just like me. Frequently our conversations and email exchanges center on Buddhist thought, but we're dudes, so our exchanges are usually only one or two paragraphs long. We're also known to meet up at the Knob Creek rifle range to shoot each other's collectible military rifles.

The world of dudes is peppered with Buddhists, but these guys don't exactly advertise their beliefs. Not like me: I have the Buddha tattooed on my left forearm. True story: I was at a gun shop once and my tattoo instigated a Dharma exchange between me, the shop owner, and the other customer in the store. We were all military veterans, and we were all serious Dharma students. Like Lance, a former tank commander who has been living in Japan for decades: he may be the toughest dude I've ever known. We go waaaaay back. These are to me more meaningful and valuable relationships because we share the bond of Buddhism. Put two or three Buddhist tough guys together in one room, and the conversation always turns to Dharma. It's a brotherhood of guys who don't run into each other very often.

You don't need to pay $900 and give up good

vacation time and hang out with nimrods in Birkenstocks to learn how to meditate. Most community Buddhist centers offer meditation classes for free or for a donation, and often, inexpensive courses in meditation are offered in adult and continuing education opportunities through colleges and public school systems. You should be suspicious of the places that make meditation out to be some otherworldly secret that only a select few can ever really gain access to (often because it's so expensive to learn!). Meditation is as simple as breathing. I can even lay the basics out for you in the next few pages. First I'll describe the physical act of "classic" calming meditation, and then I'll tell you about the stuff in your head.

I only know two people who can do the "lotus" position, my 100-pound Vietnamese Zen Master buddy and a hyperactive fifth-grader who seems like he's made out of rubber. Unless you work for Cirque du Soleil, forget the lotus position. Many an American knee has been ruined trying. If you're old, fat, and/or arthritic (like me), there's nothing wrong with meditating in a straight-backed chair (La-Z-Boys don't count), or on a park bench, or on a convenient stump. Most younger and more limber meditators sit Indian-style on a nice fat cushion of some sort, something just high enough to elevate the butt, prevent knee strain, and keep their legs from falling asleep too quickly. If you do sit Indian-style, though, try to have your ankles uncrossed, one in front of the other. Old, fat, arthritic guys who still want to sit cross-legged need something a bit higher and a whole lot more stable. My personal favorite meditation seat is made for and marketed to turkey hunters. It's a black aluminum frame that folds out to about five inches tall, topped with a square, three-inch-thick waterproof cushion rendered in Mossy Oak° camouflage. It even has a shoulder strap for easy transport.

Once you've got your butt settled, there is the matter of what to do with the rest of your body. You need to sit up as straight as you can with

The second your brain has "nothing" to do,
we find out how difficult it really is to shut off
the streaming jumble of thoughts that zing
around inside our heads.

your chest out, just like they teach you in band camp. Even sitting straight, you should have a slight forward curve in your lower back, the top of the pelvis tilted a little forward. Shoulders relaxed (people overlook this, but it's important to relieve the tension in your shoulders), with your arms hanging naturally and your hands resting on your thighs. Keep your head straight and your eyes 30 percent open. If you close your eyes all the way, you'll fall asleep. I cheat on this rule all the time, but apart from the time I started snoring at the Vipassana Society, I haven't really embarrassed myself in public. Some instructors suggest thinking of yourself as a puppet hanging from a single string attached to the top of your head with a little eyebolt. (OK. Hardware embellishments are my own. This is a book for guys who watch *Caddyshack* at least once a year.)

Now comes the hard part. *Breathe.*

Breathe naturally. Don't speed up, slow down, or make yourself breathe deeper or shallower. Just breathe. Pay attention to what you are doing, namely breathing. Observe your breath closely. If you relax your belly a bit, you can feel the rise and fall of your abdomen. Notice the air from your breath in your mustache. Feel your inhalation at the bottom of your nostrils, and the exhalation at the tops. Hear the sound of your breath going in and out of your bronchial tubes. Concentrate!

Life is like breath. All things come and go, rise and fall. Everything about life is impermanent. You're a different person than you were before you read this chapter. You are a different person from the one you were last year, yesterday, before lunch. But don't think about that now! Breathe.

It is nearly impossible not to think, especially for beginning meditators. Meditation teachers call this "monkey mind," because your thoughts jump all over the place. When you catch your-self thinking, just blow it off and return to your breath.

The most advanced meditator I know is a Zen master Vietnamese monk who tells beginning meditators to count their breaths in their head, starting with one and counting to ten and then counting back down to one again. For people who are only beginning to meditate, this simple mental act is infuriatingly difficult to accomplish. But you're not sitting on this pillow to piss yourself off, so blow it off and start counting again from one. Trust me, it'll come. Don't make more out of your initial frustration than it's worth. Everybody goes through this.

Blow it off and try again.

Oh, shit! I'm thinking again!

Blow it off.

These are the basics of calming meditation. In general, this "classic" type of meditation is all about concentration and focus, and it makes up the basis on which more in-depth meditations are developed.

Now comes the cool part. When you ground your meditation practice with a little wisdom (see everything above), you begin the process of another type of meditation known as "insight" meditation. Thoughts, like everything else, are ephemeral. They rise and fall like your breaths. And after all, they're only thoughts. They count less than a healthy fart. Initially, you'll be plagued by thoughts of things that seem very important to you. *Where the hell am I going to find the money to buy my squeeze the Christmas present she deserves? Christ, this pain is never going to go away. I lost a leg in Anbar Province. What if Mom doesn't survive the operation?*

Dude, *they're only thoughts*, and you don't need to entertain them at the same time you're supposed to be counting your breaths. One... two... *MAN, MY BOSS IS A PAIN IN THE ASS!*

When you see the truth and learn to be a little more forgiving of yourself and more objective about life in general, you'll be able to blow off even the most dire of ruminant thoughts, seeing them for what they are—just thoughts! Think later. Right now you're supposed to be counting your breaths.

Anything can be blown off. My dad survived

the Chosin Reservoir and the Tet Offensive and never lost a step. Now that he's eighty-five, he's starting to talk about the things he never talked about before. Every new story I hear makes it more and more incredible to me that he is such a sweet, generous, helpful, and gentle man. Dad is a very self-disciplined man, and he's worked hard to discipline his thoughts. I don't want to disparage or think lightly of the suffering of anyone. But given a little time, you find that some thoughts are not demons, they're monkeys. They only turn into rabid *Wizard of Oz* monkeys if you let them.

As we deal with the thoughts that pop up during meditation, we gain the insight that we can be real drama queens in our heads. I remember having random thoughts that jolted me physically and even caused rushes of adrenaline, and violent rages I quelled with three or four seconds of closed-eye time and a nice deep breath. When you realize that a thought is only a thought, you can see it for what it is, look at it, and dispense with it. And as we learn to do that in meditation, we begin to see that our minds are doing that even when we aren't meditating. It is this way of seeing things that is called "insight." And it is insight that strengthens and deepens our wisdom and helps us keep our cool even when the shit hits the fan.

Start with five minutes of sitting meditation and gradually increase the time, within reason, as you begin to feel the benefits of what you're doing. Over time, you'll probably start to find you're able to do this more and more without getting distracted by random thoughts or itchy balls.

11
OK, This Is Really Important

The ultimate realization you must come to is the very hardest one for most people of a "Western" mindset to make: there is no enduring, stable "self." Buddhists refer to this idea, simply enough, as the concept of "no-self" (or *anatta*, in Buddhist lingo). Once you can start to appreciate this notion, the sky's the limit. Actually, it's not even the limit. You can achieve more personal fulfillment than you ever imagined.

In the West, the individual is paramount. You are the center of your universe. You are who you are, and you are somebody special. If you were born after 1964 you probably got trophies just for showing up. Among the things you take into consideration as you wend your way through life is how things will affect *you*. As you pass a home-less person on the street, you're disturbed by his presence and you think, "If I make eye contact with him, he'll ask me for money," not "Boy, that man must be really suffering" or "What can I do to help?" Concern for ourselves motivates much of what we think and do. *What's in it for me? Do I really want to do this? Where do I fit in? What do they really think of me? Do they like me? Do these pants make my butt look big? I'm not putting up with that crap anymore! I know salmon is sup-posed to be good for you, but please don't make it every week. Jesus, my knees hurt.*

I like to think that most people are not self-centered and egotistical and only out for them-selves. Generally, people don't care for the company of others who think way too much of themselves. The sociopaths, the Bernie Madoffs of the world, are the extremes, not the mean. Most of us, in other words, are good guys who strike an uneasy balance when it comes to think-ing about what's good for us and what's good for others. Buddhism releases you from that ambiguity by helping you to realize that who you are, or who you consider yourself to be, is basically only a mindset, a mental formation, an *idea* of who you are. Your consciousness is ever evolving. Your identity is not unchangeable or immutable. In fact it changes all the time. Talk to a business executive sidelined by a heart attack and you'll know what I mean.

Ultimately your ego prevents you from becoming free. Here I don't just mean that self-importance is a trap. I mean that your very sense of yourself as distinct and totally independent from others holds you back. That doesn't mean that you are only a figment of your imagination. What it does mean is that we take ourselves too seriously, and the less important we perceive ourselves to be when compared to others, the freer we are to accomplish great things. You are a part of the fabric of existence. You are embedded in society as surely as your pancreas is embedded in you. You're not the action, you're a piece of the action. The less self-important you feel, the more you focus on how what you do affects those around you; the more you focus on how you affect those around you, the more *effective* you become as a person.

Parenting is a good analogy for the no-self thing. Things change when you become a parent, and you find yourself making lifestyle changes and personal sacrifices on behalf of your children. *No more Heineken! Baby needs a new pair of shoes, so it's back to Old Milwaukee Light for you, pops. It's OK, dear, we can go to Vegas again after little Matilda leaves for college.* Under duress good parents defend their children with a ferocity they never believed they were capable of. Buddhism helps you see yourself mounting that level of defense for all other people.

Get the picture? Your paradigm needs to shift away from yourself and in the direction of others. The ultimate act of renunciation, the giving up of possessiveness, clinging, and irrational desire, is to lose *yourself*. That doesn't mean that you can't own a motorboat. But how much motorboat do you need? Adopting the Buddhist concept of no-self means, practically speaking, that you generally always think of others and of the greater good before you think of yourself. If you're a veteran, especially Army or Marines, you know all about that. That's the way they trained you.

Do you want to know why the Dalai Lama is always grinning like a raccoon? Because he realizes that ultimately, he's no more important than anyone else.

I think it's sad that people quest for spirituality because they think it will make them special, when the opposite is true: True happiness comes when you realize just how special you aren't.

12
The Real Secret of Life

Hang in there! If you stick with meditation, before too long it becomes a pleasure, something you look forward to. Eventually it can become as much a part of your life as eating or watching TV. When you get past the point of having to count ten breaths up and down before some stupid thought pops into your head, then you know that you're starting to reap the mental and physical benefits of your practice. And as your ability to concentrate on your breathing improves, the benefits of meditation start to show.

The first thing I noticed was that I was generally less stressed. Physiologically, you're teaching yourself how to relax in a meaningful way, and that is good for your heart. When you meditate,

My day always begins with ten minutes
of sitting meditation with my jammy bottoms
down around my ankles.

your heart rate slows down, your blood pressure drops, and muscular tension is eased. Your brain relaxes and rests, and your energy is restored. At the same time, the wisdom that Buddhist thought lends to the process allows you to understand that "stress" really comes from how you see and react to certain situations. As you develop mental discipline, you come to be better able to choose the way you respond to things. The objectivity that reflection and meditation on Buddhist teachings bring tells you that it is ignorant to react hastily, without a second thought.

Take road rage. Some clown comes speeding around you on the highway and then cuts uncomfortably close in front of you to hit his exit. Does that have to be infuriating? You're still going to have to slow down, whether you're furious or not, so why get pissed off to begin with? Take a one-breath meditation and turn your rage into humor. *That poor schmuck must be about to pee his pants!*

The small realization that you don't have to react uncontrollably to circumstances that piss you off can be built upon in ways that let you finally deal with thoughts that continually disturb your peace of mind. Most of us have them. (If you don't, then you're blessed.) Maybe you saw your buddy blown apart in an IED blast, or your house is in abatement and you're afraid that you're about to lose everything. Your wife has cancer. *You* have cancer. Your boss is a sadistic jerk. You were in an auto accident. The city has condemned your property so they can build a new sports arena. You miss your ex-wife and kids, and now you regret the affairs you had, not just getting caught. Your kid uses heroin. You're depressed. You're in prison for the next ten years. You can't afford the surgery to stop the pain.

Being a Buddhist changes none of these things. It helps you better deal with them. It provides you with the knowledge and understanding to put things in perspective, and it offers mechanisms to redirect your thoughts and emotions at will. Buddhism affirms that even under the worst of circumstances, there are still opportunities to do things that will make you happy.

Mastering your mind is about mastering your emotions. From a Buddhist perspective, even good emotions are bad for you, because they can reinforce craving and desire. That doesn't mean you don't *have* emotions; after all, that's part of being human. And that doesn't mean that you can't passionately love your wife or wear a "cheese-head" hat to the football stadium or buy a fishing boat. It's about putting positive emotions in proper perspective and not being controlled by negative emotions. Who are you really hurting when you indulge in rage? Only yourself, of course. So, really, dude, why do it? Likewise, who are you really helping when you do something to make someone else happy without thinking about yourself? Both of you! So, really, dude, why not do it?

It's wisdom that dispels bad emotions, and it's through meditation that you develop the mental muscle to be able to blow off anger, hatred, and grief. Wisdom is a good thing and so is meditation, but when you put the two together, then you've really got something.

I love that old song "Make Someone Happy." I especially like the Jimmy Durante version. The secret of life is in that song.

13
Roadside Attractions

If you meet the Buddha on the road, kill him!
—ZEN MASTER LINJI

My intention in this little book has been to
inform you about the Buddhist path. I hope that
while doing so, I've helped you become interested in learning more. There's a lot of good
material out there about Buddhism, and there
are plenty of Buddhist societies and temples
run by wise instructors. If you do want further
information, just remember that some sources
are better than others. Recall that the Buddha
insisted on skepticism, even about what he himself said, so in the end, you'll have to trust your
own wits. Be especially wary if there are high

costs involved in leading you to enlightenment. The Dharma is free.

Buddhism is not about vegetarianism, animal rights, peace activism, politics, being green, or acting smug. It is about dealing with the world and yourself with truth and honesty, the development of a mind superior in wisdom and focused on the moment, and a sense of rightness about your role in life. It's about being happy and helping others with compassion and generosity, and realizing that ultimately, they are one and the same thing. It is about cultivating fearlessness.

There are a lot of people out there who insist that they're Buddhists but can't tell the Eightfold Path from a wet sidewalk. There are also a lot of people out there—regular dudes—who know and live the Dharma. You might not know that they're Buddhist until they tell you so, or unless, like me, they have the Buddha tattooed on themselves in a conspicuous place. I know Buddhist cops, businessmen, production workers, and even Buddhist military personnel. They're content, well-adjusted, dependable guys (and a few women sailors). They might be a little quiet, but they smile a lot.

Monks are much easier to spot given that they wear their beliefs on their sleeves, so to speak. Monks are happy to talk to you when you meet one in public. I met one in Key West not long ago at a bus stop, and he gave me a little amulet I now wear around my neck. You can usually trust monks. They are expected to live up to a standard in which the Five Precepts are only a warm-up. Although there are American monks out there, the majority will be from Buddhist countries, like Vietnam, Thailand, Laos, Cambodia, and Burma in Southeast Asia, Tibet and Sri Lanka in South Asia, and China, Taiwan, and Japan in East Asia. Immigrant communities from Buddhist countries tend to have a monk or two in them. If you want to meet a monk, ask the owner of your favorite Thai restaurant.

You can read about Buddhism until you're as blue in the face as a Hindu deity, but interacting with knowledgeable, sincere Buddhist practitioners will help you bring what you read more sensibly into your life. Monks are often a great resource as living exemplars of life dedicated to practice. Not only can they teach you about Buddhism, they can also connect you with other dudes who are on the path. Once you get to know some of them, you've joined a pretty exclusive fraternity.

They're not that hard to find, but remember: Buddhism doesn't come to you. You have to go to Buddhism. From your very first step as a Dharma dude, you've got to put some effort into it. Buddhist writer Steven Batchelor said it quite well in his excellent book *Buddhism Without Beliefs*: "Buddhism isn't something to believe in, Buddhism is something to do."

So, really, dude, put on your big girl panties, shut your pie hole, go down to the gift shop in Chinatown, buy yourself a Buddha statue, put it somewhere where you'll see it often, hitch up your jeans, and face reality head on. It is what it is.

If you're grounded in the present moment, then the past has no power, and the future doesn't exist!

Acknowledgments

I would like to thank first and foremost my wife Phyllis, the Christian exemplar of my life, who patiently supports, through my many failures, all my efforts to try to do good. Also Lance Gatling, Graham Snowden, and Linda Blanchard, of Tokyo, London, and Midland, Texas, respectively, for suggestions regarding the content of *Buddhism for Dudes*.

Over the course of my research I have found the writings of three sages most informative and inspiring: the late Walpola Rahula, Bikkhu Bodhi, and Thich Nhat Hanh. Thanks to the Dalai Lama, who presents to the world the real face of Buddhism, the happy face.

And to my teachers: Mrs. Carminie Samarasinghe, Ven. D.W. Pemarathana, Ven. Omalpe Sobhita Thero, Ven. Embilipitiya Nanda Thero, the honorable W.J.M. Lokubandara, and Master Ven. Thich Hang Dat.

I owe an enormous debt of gratitude to the villagers of Randeniya, Sri Lanka, my little jungle village, among whom I felt like I was around my own people for the first time in my life; also to the Millennium Elephant Foundation and the Sri Bodhiraja Foundation.

I would especially like to recognize the contributions of my editor at Wisdom Publications, Andy Francis. Guiding a stubborn old jarhead like me through the process of publishing *Buddhism for Dudes* must have been quite a chore.

Gerry Stribling
Louisville, Kentucky

About the Author

Gerry Stribling was born in 1951 at Fort Reilly, Kansas, to parents who were both in the military. He enlisted in the U.S. Marine Corps in 1970 and has had careers in teaching and human services. Today he volunteers for Hosparus of Louisville where, in his words, he is witnessing the final chapter of World War II.

Stribling studied Buddhism in Sri Lanka with the Venerable D. W. Pemarathana, the Venerable Omalpe Sobhita Thero, and the Hon. W. J. M. Lokubandara. In August 2003, Gerry was given the title of Dhammadutta, lay teacher of Dharma. Stribing occasionally leads small discussion groups and teaches the Buddhadharma one-on-one for free to anyone who wants to learn.

About Wisdom Publications

WISDOM PUBLICATIONS is the leading publisher of contemporary and classic Buddhist books and practical works on mindfulness. Publishing books from all major Buddhist traditions, Wisdom is a nonprofit charitable organization dedicated to cultivating Buddhist voices the world over, advancing critical scholarship, and preserving and sharing Buddhist literary culture.

To learn more about us or to explore our other books, please visit our website at wisdompubs.org. You can subscribe to our eNewsletter, request a print catalog, and find out how you can help support Wisdom's mission either online or by writing to:

Wisdom Publications
199 Elm Street
Somerville, Massachusetts 02144 USA

You can also contact us at 617-776-7416 or info@wisdompubs.org.

Wisdom is a 501(c)(3) organization, and donations in support of our mission are tax deductible.

Wisdom Publications is affiliated with the Foundation for the Preservation of the Mahayana Tradition (FPMT).

More Books from Wisdom Publications

Saltwater Buddha

A Surfer's Quest to Find Zen on the Sea

"Heartfelt, honest, and deceptively simple."—Alex Wade, author of *Surf Nation*

Hardcore Zen

Punk Rock, Monster Movies, and the Truth about Reality

"Entertaining, bold, and refreshingly direct, this book is likely to change the way one experiences other books about Zen—and maybe even the way one experiences reality."—*Publishers Weekly* starred review

The Dharma of Star Wars

"A Buddhist interpretation of the Jedi Way. This entertaining and insightful primer provides a useful service to film buffs who want to better understand the real-life religion behind this fictional world."—*Tricycle*

Money, Sex, War, Karma

Notes for a Buddhist Revolution

"Revolutionary! The clear and concise explanations of Buddhist perspectives on rarely approached topics are an inspiration. If you are interested in personal or societal change, this is a book you need to read."—Noah Levine, author of *Against the Stream* and *Dharma Punx*

Walking the Way
81 Zen Encounters with the Tao Te Ching

"Rosenbaum manages to restore some of the bite to the Tao Te Ching. His humor, wisdom, personal failings, and genuine aspirations combine to make it new."—Barry Magid, author of *Ending the Pursuit of Happiness*

Bad Dog!
A Memoir of Love, Beauty, and Redemption in Dark Places

"It reads like something Steinbeck might have written had he been a Buddhist, and I can pay an author no higher compliment."—Christopher Moore, author of *A Dirty Job*